SOVIET
VISUALS

SOVIET VISUALS

VARIA BORTSOVA

BLOOMSBURY PUBLISHING

LONDON • OXFORD • NEW YORK • NEW DELHI • SYDNEY

I dedicate this book to the two people who have taught me to see humour and beauty in everything and without whom this entire project would have never happened: my parents Olga and Sergey

CONTENTS

INTRODUCTION

In true spirit of the widespread Soviet economic practice of counter-planning, my first encounter with the USSR took place a little earlier than expected. My soon-to-be mother was in her eighth month of pregnancy when her state-run maternity hospital in the east of Moscow announced that it was closing down for 'sanitation procedures' and gently requested that she (and the other women) please hurry up. One induced labour, and I was born into the USSR – just in time, as a few pivotal historical events later, the Soviet Union collapsed after seventy years of existence. The once largest country in the world was no more, replaced by fifteen different nations and a complex and muddled jigsaw puzzle of shared identities, cultures and visual artefacts left behind.

After discovering my parents' archive of home videos and cassettes, I became fascinated with collecting the remnants of this era – expanding my quest to libraries, friends of friends' photo albums and obscure flea markets. Every awkward wedding snapshot, television recording and carefully folded fashion catalogue page is, in a way, a glimpse into the lives of nearly 300 million Soviet people as they experienced love and pain, celebrated their children's birthdays, joined the (only) party, laughed, cried and dreamed in sanatoriums, prisons, communal kitchens and highly sought-after automobiles.

In May 2016, I decided to start a Twitter account called Soviet Visuals to consolidate these makeshift archives for a small group of friends. As it grew, the page evolved into a community of people contributing their own photographs, videos and personal stories as well as curious observers from all parts of the world.

For some, the project embodies the nostalgic aftertaste of a shared past; for others, a sneak peek behind the Iron Curtain and an opportunity to reflect critically on the social and cultural norms of the time. The project is in no way an attempt to glorify or justify the USSR's ideological constructs and totalitarian practices; I deeply sympathise with the victims of the numerous horrors and brutalities of the Soviet system. It is, however, important to acknowledge the various elements of propaganda that were woven into the fabric of Soviet citizens' everyday lives, as seen in many of the visuals.

For me, the greatest appeal is in unearthing certain trivial elements of Soviet people's day-to-day existence: some questionable fashion choices, a ridiculously graphic factory safety poster, the peculiar design of a home appliance, a long-forgotten regional pop star…

One of the most rewarding aspects of curating these images has been the opportunity to observe the kinds of reactions and conversations that they prompt in people. Some are to be expected, but many have taken me by surprise: for example, the sheer number of enthusiastic reactions to a 1970s photograph of somebody's very good-looking grandfather which *almost* broke the internet (page 73), or the time a man reached out to ask if he could open an account called Soviet Azerbaijan (of course you can, I told him … this is social media, not the Soviet Union!).

While no amount of photographs can fully capture the multi-layered realities of Soviet society, each image in this book was chosen after careful deliberation, and my hope is that they inspire you to explore further, to question and look beyond the obvious.

SCIENCE AND TECHNOLOGY

'Granny said sternly: don't go anywhere without God. But the bright light of science proved that there is no God!', anti-religion poster, 1965

'Soyuz-Apollo', poster by Lubsan Dorzhiev depicting
the first international space mission, 1976

Young Cosmonauts Club at the Young Pioneer camp
in Orlyonok, Krasnodar region, 1979

MY SOVIET VISUAL

This photo shows the happiest time of our family life. We are on Baku boulevard in the summer of 1983: my mother and father are together, and I am riding a pedal car, my favourite childhood entertainment. The car was not mine; at the time, you could rent one for 20 pennies an hour. Now, most children have this kind of car at home, even electric ones, but the ones back then were quite difficult to ride, with heavy metal pedals. My father says they were better, because they taught children about hard work and effort.

My parents got divorced seven years after this photo was taken. I was ten then, it was a painful time both for the family and the country as it coincided with the dissolution of the Soviet Union.

My parents got acquainted and loved each other when they studied in the choral faculty of an academic music college in the 1970s. They are both musicians. And I grew up to be a novelist and philosophy teacher. My mother tore up all of the old family photos of those times with my father in them. She wanted to tear up this photo too. But I was able to save it.

via Nermin Kamal

Вдруг стали вес они терять,
Вдруг стали, как пушинки.
· Им на ногах не устоять —
Они плывут на спинке.

Повисла в воздухе вода.
Плывёт пустая кружка.
И Стрелка взвизгнула:
— Беда!
Держи меня, подружка!

Illustration from a children's book about Soviet
space dogs Belka and Strelka, 1962

Soviet space dogs Belka and Strelka pose for
a photo after their return from space, 1960

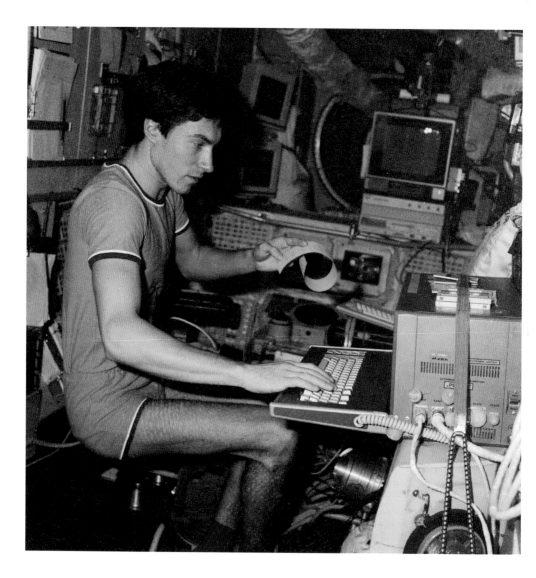

Alexey Leonov and Deke Slayton on the Apollo-Soyuz
space mission, 1975

Cosmonaut Sergey Krikalev inputs information on
completed experiments into the Zora computer, 1988

Computer laboratory at the Department of Applied Mathematics,
Lenin State University, Dushanbe, Tajik SSR, 1976

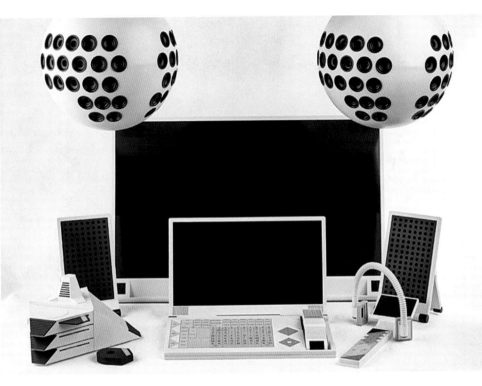

Concept design for a home automation system,
Sphinx project, 1987

Control room, Metsamor Nuclear Power Plant,
Armenian SSR, 1980s

Soviet vision of the future for Moscow, illustration, 1930s

'Be careful when pulling wires' Soviet work safety poster, 1929

'Duel', Moscow State University, 1963

'I'll become a chemist!', poster, 1964

WORKERS IN RUSSIA, CAN'T THEY FLY IN SPACE?'

VALENTINA TERESHKOVA, first woman in space

ПЛАНЕТОХОД-ФАНТАЗИЯ
«ГАГАРИНЕЦ» СОЗДАН
ЮНЫМИ ТЕХНИКАМИ
ГОРОДА СУМЫ.
ЕГО КОНСТРУКТОРЫ
ЗАВОЕВАЛИ ГЛАВНЫЙ ПРИЗ
IX ВСЕСОЮЗНОГО КОНКУРСА
«КОСМОС» — КУБОК
ЖУРНАЛА.

МОДЕЛИСТ 1979·7
КОНСТРУКТОР

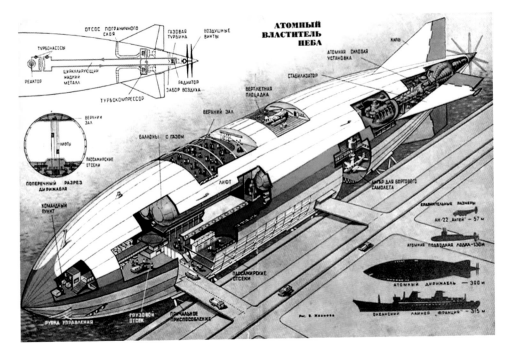

‘Atomic ruler of the sky’, illustration of an atomic
airship, 1971

Cover of *Modelist Konstruktor*, a monthly practical
hobbyist magazine, 1979

Passenger snowmobile, 1968

Soviet backpack propeller aero-engine MPI, 1967

Inventor Boris Grishin, and
his automatic radio-electronic
secretary (ARS) robot, 1966

First robot design contest,
Kaliningrad, 1969

Sheremetyevo International Airport,
Moscow, 1974

Homeland, your task is completed! poster, 1969

FASHION
AND
DESIGN

Models showcasing a
fashion collection, 1988

Spring in Leningrad, painting by Andrei Sinitsa, 1987

First Miss Soviet Union
beauty pageant, 1988

Model Galina Milovskaya
photographed for *Vogue*
Paris by Arnaud De
Rosnay, 1969

MY SOVIET VISUAL

This photo was taken in one of the two major parks in Lvov in the winter of either 1962 or 1963. There is this song we kids used to sing, in a blank verse translation:

In a stone cavern we found a thimble of vodka,

And a fried mosquito lay on the frying pan.

(But that's not enough vodka, not enough vodka,
and also not enough zakuska [the Russian equivalent
of an hors d'oeuvre].)

In a stone cavern we found a bottle of vodka,

And a fried chicken lay on the frying pan.

(Refrain)

In a stone cavern we found a barrel of vodka/
a fried boar ...

Cistern/mammoth ...

In a stone cavern we found a spring of vodka,

A herd of mammoth grazed on the frying pan,

But there isn't enough vodka,

And also not enough zakuska.

via Anatoly Belilovsky

Winners of the All-Union
"Fashion" magazine prize,
1989

Actress Zinaida Reich
as Phosphoric Woman in
Vladimir Mayakovsky's
play *Bath*, 1930

Official film poster for *Star Wars* (*Zvezdnye Voyny*) by Yuri Boxer and Alexander Shantsev, 1990

Models demonstrating costumes designed by Moscow artist Sergei Mikulsky, 1990

Provincial guys, 1970s

Model in *Lenigrad House of Fashion* magazine

'CREATIVITY IS AN UNENDING

'XERCISE IN UNCERTAINTY'

JOSEPH BRODSKY, Soviet poet

Alternative youth fashion, 1980s

Kharkov Girl, 1977

Poster for the film *Man with a Movie Camera*, by Vladimir and Georgy Stenberg, 1929

These two ensembles, designed by Valentina Kobtseva, are called 'The Red Devils' after a silent film about the adventurous days of the Civil War in Russia, 1967

RAF-2910, an electric minivan designed for Moscow 1980 Olympics

Volna Radio Receiver, 1961

A one-piece fur snowsuit
which traps a layer of
insulating air, Siberia, 1966

Soviet band Combo-Jazz, 1989

SPORT AND HEALTH

Morning performance at a Soviet kindergarten, 1980s

Soviet athletes at the Sapporo Winter Olympic Games, 1972

UV lamp 'light baths' were given to Soviet children in an attempt to supply them with vitamin D during winter, 1987

MY SOVIET VISUAL

This is a photo of my grandfather, Nikolay Dmitrievich Barinov, taken in the 1960s.
Sadly, he died in 1992 and I didn't get to know him. He lived somewhere in Chuvashia, and after that the family moved to the Saratov region.

Varia: This photograph of Darya's grandfather set so many hearts aflutter that it caused my Twitter app to crash on several occasions due to the sheer number of reactions and comments. Here are a few of my favourites:

'Is his shirt made by Karl Marx? Because this is causing an uprising in my lower class,' commented one Twitter follower. 'Communism means we get to share him, yes?? Yes,' was another remark. In one comment, Grandpa Nikolay was compared to a singer in an 1980s new wave band; in another, a follower confessed that she had never wanted a time machine this much in her life. Less than 24 hours after I shared the image, the post was 'liked' over a 100,000 times, beating every other visual ever posted on the account. In addition, over the next several days, the comments section (as well as my inbox) filled up with photos of other people's hot Soviet grandparents in their youth. Not the most expected turn of events, but I can't complain.

via Darya Barinova

Sports parade in Red Square, Moscow, 1938

Physical exercise break for the first-formers
of school №5, 1977

УВЕЛИЧИМ В 1951–55 гг. ЧИСЛО МЕСТ
В ДЕТСКИХ ЯСЛЯХ — НА 20%
В ДЕТСКИХ САДАХ — НА 40%

РАСТИ ЗДОРОВЫМ!

'Grow healthy!' poster, 1954

'Your health is in your hands!', poster, 1925

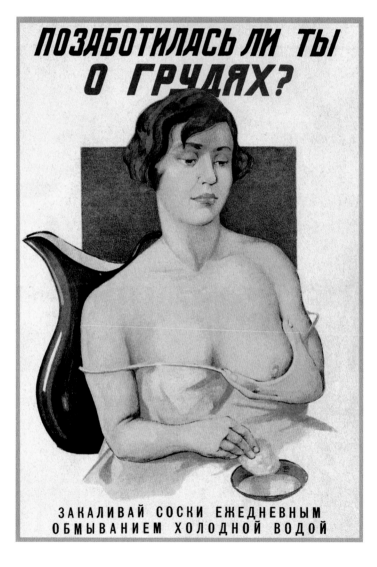

'Are you taking care of your breasts? Temper your nipples with cold water daily', poster, 1930

'Don't drink untreated water', poster, 1921

'THIS ABILITY TO CONQUER

IS NO DOUBT

THE MOST PRECIOUS OF

ONESELF

ALL THINGS SPORT

BESTOWS'

OLGA KORBUT, Olympic gymnast

'Remember about cholera. Unhygienic
practices which lead to cholera', 1921

Surgeon-otorhinolaryngologist
with colleagues, 1972

Soviet world champion finswimmer Shavarsh Karapetyan
(middle), who saved the lives of 20 people in 1976 when
he saw a trolleybus plunge into a reservoir

'Every worker athlete must be a soldier of revolution', Spartakiad poster by Gustav Klutsis, 1928

ДА ЗДРАВСТВУЕТ ВСЕСОЮЗНЫЙ ДЕНЬ ФИЗКУЛЬТУРНИКА!

'Long live the All-Union Day of the Athlete!',
poster, 1946

Gymnasts, painting by Dmitry Zhilinsky, 1965

Members of a local Polar Bear Club preparing
to take a dip in the icy Moskva River, 1961

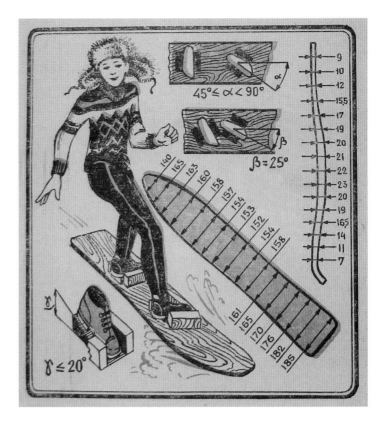

DIY snowboard, illustration from *Yuny Tekhnik*
(Young Technician) magazine supplement, 1981

Classical ballet lesson at the Moscow
Academic Ballet School, 1982

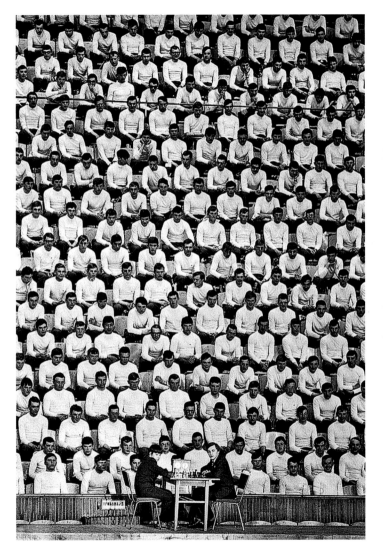

World chess champion Anatoly Karpov (seated right at the table) holds a demonstration game at the sports festival during the XVIII Komsomol Congress, 1978

The New Year celebrated in a psychiatric hospital in
Moscow, *Ogonyok* (*Little Light*) magazine, 1988

A worker and female supervisor in the Zis factory, Moscow, 1954

Workplace exercise, Moscow, 1957

'There is no place for unemployment under socialism!
Under capitalism there are millions of unemployed
hands!', poster, 1950

Hero of Socialist Labour
Valdemar Krumins, assembly
fitter with the VEF state
electro-technical plant

MY SOVIET VISUAL

This is my really cool grandma in Tbilisi, Georgia, 1979. She was a rebel, and I do not mean that she was a rebel because she wore jeans, had long hair and smoked cigarettes when nobody else did. No. She was a rebel because she believed in true democracy. Behind the Iron Curtain when everything sometimes seemed hopeless, my grandmother snuck around and read books about the United States, she listened to Churchill in quiet rooms, and at a time when everyone was hungry but she could have had a lavish life, she never gave up on her morals. She didn't join the Communist Party, even when her family was targeted and her grandfather was shot; she always had hope, hope that Georgia would soon become independent.

via Tata Tabidze

My grandmother, Arevik Hayrepetyan and her husband Aharon. The photo was taken in 1969 in Jermuk, Armenia. What makes this photo especially iconic is not only the stylish white sandals that my grandpa wore, but also the picturesque nature view and the sculpture of the deer in the background. Deer is the symbol of Jermuk.

via Aharon Hayrapetyan

Welder Lyuba Tsyganok
at the construction
of Kiev Hydroelectric
Station, 1964

A researcher of the underwater research group at the
Institute of Marine Biology holds a golden king crab, 1971

Lyudmila Rodina, employee of the Alma-Ata
children's toys factory, Kazakh SSR, 1971

Working on children's pedal cars at the
Automobile Plant named after Leninsky
Komsomol (AZLK), 1970

'We smite the pseudo-shock workers!', poster, 1931

'Comrade! Your factory is your pride', poster, 1920s

Chernobyl liquidators, 1986

'WE MUST PREPARE
NOT ONLY TO CU
BUT TO REAP

THE REAPERS,

DOWN THE TARES OF TODAY,

THE WHEAT OF TOMORROW'

VLADIMIR LENIN, leader of Soviet Russia 1917–1924

'Put Up Your Hair Under Your Headwear', work safety poster, 1989

'Night is not an obstacle for work!' poster, 1956

'Muslim worker-women! The Tsars, Beis and Khans took away your rights. You were a slave in the government, at the factory, at home. Soviet rule gave you equal rights, tearing away the chains that binded you', poster, 1921

'It would be the greatest gift for your motherland,
if you become a swineherd and set an example for
the others', poster, 1957

Post-Soviet visual, stretching out, 1993

Construction of the Moscow metro, 1950s

Construction of the main building of Moscow
State University on Lenin Hills, 1949–1953

'To trade in a civilised manner is
honourable work!', poster, 1949

Flight attendant Anaida Safaryan at Zvartnots airport, Armenian SSR, 1984

FAMILY TIME

The legendary Georgian water polo player Pyotr Mshvenieradze with his grandson, 1990s

Animal trainer Stepan Isaakyan at a
Black Sea beach, 1967

Toy cosmonauts line a shelf in the Moskva
Department Store, 1967

Doctor Igor Charkovsky doing physical exercises
with a baby at the Black Sea, 1988

MY SOVIET VISUAL

This photo was taken in February of 1981 on the outskirts of Kharkiv in Ukraine when my mother and her friends would have all been in their early twenties. My mother has always been pretty outgoing and her biggest interest was reading, she would read newspapers cover-to-cover and at the time this picture was taken had just become a school teacher, gotten married and found out she was pregnant. The friends are mostly from her school days: Sergei, on the right, was a taxi driver; Vitya, the man doing a hand gesture, was a truck driver, but passed away at a very young age from cancer; and Sasha, in the middle, was a car mechanic. She remained friends with them until 1991 when she moved to the United States.

via Gene Harlow

A child meets a baby bear
on Wrangel Island, 1975

Winter in the USSR – children in Yakutia, 1968

'A baby belongs in the nursery, not in the tundra',
poster, 1967

'Rather than scolding and beating the children,
it is better to buy them books', poster, 1928

Major Afanasy Vasilyevich Lapshov with his wife Milya and son Vova, Dnepropetrovsk, 1920s

Military commander
Semyon Buddyonny with
his son Sergei, 1940s

'A child was born', 1977

Newborn babies lie under portraits of Soviet cosmonauts in Moscow, with Gagarin's photo in the middle.

'IT'S LIKE TRYING TO FIT

INTO A PAIR OF TUXEDO

AND NOT A PLAIN

BUT AN OCTOPUS THAT

AN OCTOPUS PANTS.

OCTOPUS AT THAT,

DOESN'T EVEN EXIST'

ARKADY STRUGATSKY, *Definitely Maybe*

'My father and me', Leningrad, 1989

Gold Coast holiday resort, Georgian SSR, 1967

Waiting room at the
marriage registration
office, Tallinn, Estonian
SSR, 1973

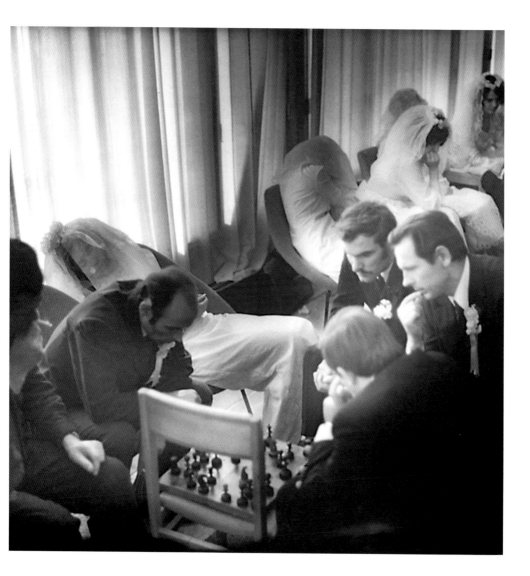

Holidaymakers in Sochi, 1981

Tourists sunbathing in
the Dombay Valley after
skiing, 1982

'Mum, dad and me', 1990s

Father and child (date unknown)

FOOD AND DRINK

Fish sellers in the market of Petropavlovsk-
Kamchatsky, Russia, 1993

Photos from *The Book of Tasty and Healthy Food*, an iconic Soviet cookbook written by scientists from the Institute of Nutrition of the Academy of Medical Sciences of the USSR, 1952 edition

Left: Sturgeon and salmon caviar

Right: Siberian meat dumplings with sour cream

Московский
ордена Ленина
Мясокомбинат
им. А.И. Микояна

СССР
ГЛАВМЯСО

Сибирские
ПЕЛЬМЕНИ

MY SOVIET VISUAL

This photo of my grandparents and aunt was taken in 1974. Five years earlier, our family moved from the village to the city. My grandmother worked as a cleaner at a university, my grandfather was a bus driver there. They both lived on campus. This photo was taken by their friend, an amateur photographer, who occasionally visited them for a cup of tea.

via Yulia Kovlekova

First McDonald's in Moscow, 1992

At a beer kiosk in Odessa, 1982

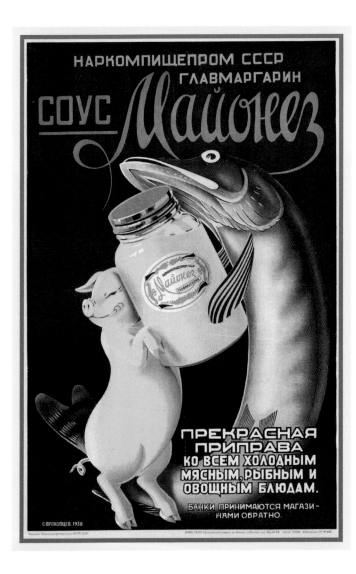

'Mayonnaise sauce. Excellent condiment for all cold meat, fish and vegetable dishes', 1938

'Full speed to corn!' poster, 1961

'Sale of mushrooms on the Danilovsky collective farm market', Moscow, 1959

'It's time for everyone to try how tasty and tender crab is', poster by the People's Commissariat for Food Industries, 1938

'There are pancakes for sale', Soviet advertising poster, 1950

'Honest work for the good of society: he who does not work, does not eat', poster, 1967

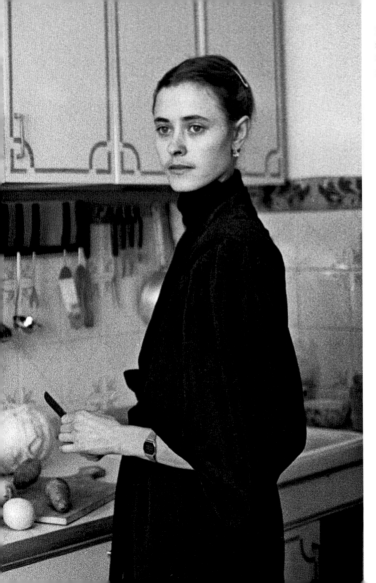

Ballerina Natalya Chekhovskaya,
soloist of the Krasnoyarsk
State Opera and Ballet Theater
preparing lunch at home, 1987

'LET THERE BE

MORE CORN AND MORE

AND LET THERE BE

NO HYDROGEN

MEAT

BOMBS AT ALL'

NIKITA KHRUSHCHEV, Premier of the Soviet Union 1958–1964

Lunch at the factory canteen, 1964

Packing caviar, Astrakhan, 1979

Malysh cafe, Tula, 1979

Children at a kindergarten,
Uzbek SSR, 1972

Mathias Rust, the German amateur pilot who astonished the world by illegally landing his Cessna in Moscow, has lunch at the court where he is standing trial. Rust was sentenced to four years in a re-education camp, 1987

Kosmos cafe, Minsk, Byelorussian SSR, 1985

ACKNOWLEDGEMENTS

I cannot express enough thanks to all the people who contributed images, feedback and advice during the the preparation of this book: my incredible family members, Sergei Vasiliev and Elizaveta Furdilova, Dmitry Azrikan, Nina Pikkel, Anatoly Belilovsky, Alex Rupin, Pascal Dumont, Georgy Mshvenieradze, Sergey Ponomarev, Anna Balala, Nika Dongarova, Denis Nesterenko, Evgenia Koshkarova, Olga Dekhanova, Artyom Kozlov, Yulia Kovlekova, Daria Barinova, Nermin Kamal, Tata Tabidze, Gene Harlow, Aharon Hayrapetyan, Dima Dewinn and countless members of the the global social media community. A special thanks to the superstars at Bloomsbury who managed to coordinate the entire process in the midst of a global pandemic: Allegra Le Fanu, Lauren Whybrow, Lesley, Genista Tate-Alexander, Jonny Coward and the team.

Finally, to all the friends and colleagues around the world who originally shared my enthusiasm at a Twitter account filled with old photographs and obscure music clips and continue to laugh at my Soviet jokes, especially the mediocre ones: I am so lucky to know you.

ILLUSTRATION CREDITS

Page 12: Reproduction of Soviet anti-religion poster by V. I. Govorkov. 'Soviet Artist' Publishing House. Author's archive.

Page 13: 'Soyuz-Apollo', illustration by Lubsan Dorzhiev, depicting the first international space mission/© Lubsan Dorzhiev 1976

Page 14-15: Photo by Valery Shustov, Krasnodar region, USSR/© Sputnik/TopFoto 1979

Page 16-17: Photo courtesy of Nermin Kamal home archive, 1983

Page 18: Illustration by B. Malinovsky from the book 'Star Travellers' by Yuri Yakovlev/© Moscow, Detsky Mir Publishing House 1962

Page 19: Photo by Sergei Preobrazhensky, Nikolai Sitnikov/© ITAR-TASS News Agency/Alamy Stock Photo

Page 20: Mir Space Station, Image by by V.Volkov/© TASS/TopFoto 1988

Page 21: Image courtesy of NASA Human Space Flight Gallery/© NASA 1975

Page 22: Image courtesy of Vatnikstan Project

Page 23: Image courtesy of Dmitry Azrikan/© Moscow Design Museum

Page 24-25: Photo by Martin Shahbazyan/© TASS/TopFoto

Page 26: Author's archive

Page 27: Author's archive

Page 28: Photo by Vsevolod Tarasevich/Courtesy of RIA Novosti archive 1963

Page 29: Poster by B. Reshetnikov 1964

Page 30-31: Photo of Valentina Tereshkova

Page 32: Cover of *Modelist Konstruktor* monthly practical hobbyist magazine, USSR 1979

Page 33: Illustration by V. Ivanov from *Technology for the Youth* magazine 1971

Page 34: Soviet backpack propeller aero-engine MPI/© TASS/TopFoto 1967

Page 35: Photo by Rudolph Alfimov/© Sputnik/TopFoto 1968

Page 36: Photo by G. Makarytchev/© Sputnik/Science Photo Library

Page 37: Kaliningrad, Scherbakov/© Sputnik/TopFoto 1969

Page 38: Photo by Vitaly Saveliev/© Sputnik/TopFoto 1974

Page 39: Poster by R. Suryaninov, 1969/Courtesy of Russian State Library 1969

Page 42: Photo by V. Gritsuk/© Sputnik/TopFoto 1988

Page 43: Painting by Andrei Sinitsa/© Andrei Sinitsa 1987

Page 44: Author's archive

Page 45: Photo by Arnaud De Rosnay, *Vogue* magazine/© Arnaud de Rosnay/Condé Nast via Getty Images 1969

Page 45: Photo by Vladimir Dotsenko/© TASS 1989

Page 46-47: Image courtesy of Anatoly Belilovsky family archive

Page 48: Photo by V. Ivleva/© Sputnik 1988

Page 49: Photo by Alexey Temerin, 1930

Page 50: Poster by Yuri Boxer and Alexander Shantsev/© Everett Collection Inc/Alamy Stock Photo 1990

Page 51: Sergei Mikulsky costume collection. Photo by A.Volodin/© Sputnik/TopFoto 1990

Page 52: Author's collection. 1970s.

Page 53: Leningrad House of Fashion Models magazine, March 1977 issue

Pages 54-55: © Getty Images

Page 56: Photo by Yuri Rupin / Courtesy of Alex Rupin 1977

Page 57: Author's collection, 1980s.

Page 58: Poster for the film *Man with a Movie Camera*, by Vladimir and Georgy Stenberg, 1929 Publisher: VUFKU (the All-Ukrainian Photo Cinema Administration), Moscow/© Universal Art Archive/Alamy Stock Photo 1929

Page 59: Fashion design by Valentina Kobtseva 1967

Page 60: RAF-2910, an electric minivan for Moscow 1980 Olympics referees, RAF (R gas Autobusu Fabrika)/ Courtesy of Thngs.co and Moscow Polytechnic Museum

Page 61: Volna Radio Receiver, 1961 Alexandov Radio Plant, Leningrad, USSR/ Courtesy of Thngs.co and Moscow Polytechnic Museum

Page 62: Photo by Dean Conger, Siberia, 1966/© Dean Conger/National Geographic Creative

Page 63: Soviet band Combo-Jazz. Photo by G.Pogorelov/© Sputnik/ TopFoto 1989

Page 66: From 'A Day in the Life of the Soviet Union' January 1, 1987 by Rick Smolan, David Cohen © Dilip Mehta/Contact Press Images/Eyevine 1987

Page 67: © The Asahi Shimbun via Getty Images 1972

Page 68-69: © Wally McNamee/CORBIS/Corbis via Getty Images

Page 70: Courtesy of Darya Barinova home archive

Page 72: Photo by Igor Gavrilov/© Sputnik/TopFoto 1977

Page 73: Physical exercise break for the first-formers of school No. 5/© Sputnik/TopFoto 1977

Page 74: Poster by G. Schubina/© State Directory of the Museum Fund of the Russian Federation 1954

Page 75: Poster by S. Yaguzhinsky; Russian Red Cross, Young Pioneer Health Service. Moscow, 1925/ Courtesy of Russian State Library

Page 76: Author's collection. Poster by P. Bekhmetyev, 1930

Page 77: : 1921. Department of Health Education of Tatar People's Commissariat of Healthcare and Kazan City Healthcare Department 1921

Page 78-79: © Alamy Stock Image

Page 80: Unhygienic practices which lead to cholera. Colour lithograph by the Ukraine Military Sanitary Directorate, Sanitary Enlightenment Department of the Kiev Region/© Wellcome Collection 1921

Page 81: Photo courtesy of Nika Dongarova family archive, 1972

Page 82: Photo by Oleg Makarov/© Sputnik/TopFoto 1983

Page 83: Postcard for the All Union Spartakiada Sporting Event by Gustav Klucis, 1928/© New York Museum of Modern Art (MoMA) 2020. Digital image, The Museum of Modern Art, New York/Scala, Florence

Page 84: Reproduction of painting by Dmitry Zhilinsky/ Courtesy of Sputnik Images 1965

Page 85: 'Long live the All-Union Day of the Athlete!' Soviet poster 1946/ Poster image provided by Poster Plakat.com 1946

Page 86: Photo by Carl Mydans/© The *LIFE* Picture Collection via Getty Images 1961

Page 87: Illustration from *Yuny Tekhnik* (Young Technician) magazine supplement, 1981

Page 88: Photo by Alexander Makarov/© Sputnik/TopFoto 1982

Page 89: Photo by Vladimir Rodionov, 1978

Page 90-91: Photo by Pavel Krivtsov, Moscow, *Ogonyok* magazine 1988

Page 94: © Henri Cartier-Bresson / Magnum Photos 1954

Page 95: Photo by Jerry Cooke/© Jerry Cooke Archive 1957

Page 96: Poster by V. Koretskii/© State Directory of the Museum Fund of the Russian Federation 1950

Page 97: © Sputnik/TopFoto 1972

Page 98-99: Photo courtesy of Tata Tibidze family archive/Photo courtesy of the Aharon Hayrapetyan family archive

Page 100: Photo by Mikhail Kuleshov/© Sputnik/TopFoto 1964

Page 101: Photo by Yuri Somov/© Sputnik/TopFoto

Page 102: Photo by S. Solovyov / © Sputnik/TopFoto 1970

Page 103: Photo by Iosif Budnevich, Kazakh SSR/© Sputnik/ TopFoto 1971

Page 104: *Fighting Lazy Workers*, 1931/© New York, Museum of Modern Art (MoMA). Gift of Miss Jessie Rosenfeld © 2020. Digital image, The Museum of Modern Art, New York/Scala, Florence

Page 105: Berlin, Scientific and technical department of VSNKh Bint, R. Barnik/© Peffer 1920s.

Page 106: B. Krishtul/© Sputnik/TopFoto 1967

Page 107: Photo by Valery Zufarov, USSR/© TASS/TopFoto 1986

Page 108-109: © Getty Images

Page 110: Poster by S.N.Orlov, 1989. Author's archive.

Page 111: Author's collection. Reproduction of poster by B. Reshetnikov, 1962.

Page 112: Author unknown. Baku, 1921/© Mardjani Foundation 1921

Page 113: V. Rougeau [Smolensk]: Smol, book publishing house, c. 1957. Courtesy of Russian State Library archive

Page 114-115: Photo by Sergei Mamontov, Gennady Khamelyanin/© TASS/TopFoto 1993

Page 116: Moscow, USSR. 24 November 1948. Moscow Metro under construction. A view of a double-track tunnel at Paveletskaya station under construction/© Leonid Velikzhanin/TASS/TopFoto

Page 117: The construction of the main building of Moscow State University on Lenin Hills/© Heritage-Images/TopFoto

Page 118: Poster by Viktor Iwanovich Govorkov. Colour lithograph/© Russian State Library archive, Moscow 1949

Page 119: Photo by Fred Grinberg, Yerevan, Armenian SSR/© Sputnik/TopFoto 1984

Page 122: Author's archive, 1990s. Permission courtesy of Georgy Mshvenieradze

Page 123: Photo by Yuri Somov/© TASS/Sputnik/TopFoto 1967

Page 124: Photo by Alexander Grashchenkov © Sputnik/TopFoto 1988

Page 125: © Bettmann/Contributor 1967 via Getty Images

Page 126-127: Photo courtesy of Gene Harlow family archive

Page 128: 1975 Wrangel Island, Chukotka, Siberia, 1975. Photo by Georgy Nadezhdin/© TASS/TopFoto

Page 129: 'They live in Yakutia'. Photo by Aleksandr Gostev, *Soviet Photo* magazine, January 1968 issue

Page 130: 1967 poster by B.E. Teders. Ministry of Healthcare of the RSFSR/© Russian State Library archive 1967

Page 131: Poster by N. Pomansky, Centrosoyuz 1928

Page 132: Photo courtesy of Denis Nesterenko and the Lapshov family archive (https://lapshov.su/)

Page 133: Photographer unknown, 1940s

Page 134: Photo courtesy of Sergey Vasilyev and Elizaveta Furdilova, 1977

Page 135: Moscow. USSR. Newborn children lying under portraits of Soviet cosmonauts/© TASS/TopFoto 1963

Page 136-137: © Sputnik/Alamy Stock Photo

Page 138: Photo © Igor Kostin, 1986

Page 139: Photo courtesy of Artyom Kozlov family archive

Page 140: Irakli Chokhonelidze/© TASS/TopFoto 1967

Page 141: Photographer unknown. Tallinn, Estonian SSR, 1973.

Page 142: © Peter Marlow/Magnum Photos 1981

Page 143: Photo by Yuri Somov /© Sputnik/TopFoto 1982

Page 144: Photo courtesy of Olga Dekhanova family archive, 1990s

Page 145: Date and photographer unknown. Photo courtesy of Nina Pikkel archive

Page 148-149: Petropavlovsk-Kamchatsky © Reuters 1993

Page 150: Illustration from *The Book of Tasty and Healthy Food* (Книга о вкусной и здоровой пище, Kniga o vkusnoi i zdorovoi pishche), 1952 edition. Collective work (Institute of Nutrition of the Academy of Medical Scientists of the USSR)/© Azoor Photo/Alamy Stock Photo 1952

Page 151: Illustration from *The Book of Tasty and Healthy Food* (Книга о вкусной и здоровой пище, Kniga o vkusnoi i zdorovoi pishche), 1952 edition. Collective work (Institute of Nutrition of the Academy of Medical Scientists of the USSR)/© Azoor Photo/Alamy Stock Photo 1952

Page 152-153: Picture courtesy of Yulia Kovlekova family archive

Page 154: McDonalds, Moscow, 1992/© Martin Parr/Magnum Photos 1992

Page 155: Men buying beer from a kiosk to drink on the street in the city/© Ian Berry/Magnum Photos

Page 156: 1938 advertising poster by S.S. Prokoptsev. Author's archive.

Page 157: 1964 billboard poster. Photograph by Jacques Dupâquier

Page 158: Photo by B. Anthony Stewart, Moscow, USSR/© B. Anthony Stewart/National Geographic Creative 1959

Page 159: People's Commissariat for Food Industry of the USSR: Glavryba. Poster by A. A. Miller – Moscow: Soyuzpishchepromreklama/© Russian State Library Archive 1938

Page 160: Advertising poster by V. Grevsky. Author's archive.

Page 161: 1967 poster by Nikolai Babin and Georgii Gausman/© 'Soviet Artist' Publishing House 1967

Page 162-163: 22 August 1987 Ballet soloist of the Krasnoyarsk State Ballet and Opera Theatre Natalya Chekhovskaya makes dinner at home. Fred Grinberg/© Sputnik/TopFoto

Page 164-165: © Getty Images

Page 166: USSR, 6 January 1964. Lunch at the factory canteen/© TASS/TopFoto 1964

Page 167: Caviar packing in caviar shop floor, Caspian caviar-balyk production association/© akg-images/Sputnik 1973

Page 168: 1979, Photo courtesy of 'Tula in Past' project.

Page 169: © Klaus Rose/ullstein bild via Getty Images

Page 170: Photo by Yuri Abramochkin, USSR/© Tass/TopFoto 1987

Page 171: Author's archive. Photographer unknown.

BLOOMSBURY PUBLISHING
Bloomsbury Publishing Plc
50 Bedford Square, London, WC1B 3DP, UK

BLOOMSBURY, BLOOMSBURY PUBLISHING and the Diana logo are trademarks of
Bloomsbury Publishing Plc

First published in Great Britain 2020

A catalogue record for this book is available from the British Library

ISBN: HB: 978-1-5266-2840-4; eBook: 978-1-5266-2841-1

10 9 8 7 6 5 4 3 2

Project Editors: Lauren Whybrow and Allegra Le Fanu
Designer: Daniel New

Printed and bound in Germany by Mohn Media

To find out more about our authors and books visit www.bloomsbury.com and sign up
for our newsletters